W9-CQG-614

YOUNG PROFILES

Britney Spears

Tamara L. Britton
ABDO Publishing Company

HESTLER
Library Media Center

Grant Academy Library
470 E. Jackson Street
San Jose, CA 95112

visit us at
www.abdopub.com

Published by ABDO Publishing Company 4940 Viking Drive, Edina, Minnesota 55435.
Copyright © 2000 by Abdo Consulting Group, Inc. International copyrights reserved in
all countries. No part of this book may be reproduced in any form without written
permission from the publisher.

Printed in the United States.

Photo credits: AP/Wide World

Edited by Paul Joseph

Library of Congress Cataloging-in-Publication Data

Britton, Tamara L., 1963-
      Britney Spears / Tamara L. Britton.
        p. cm. -- (Young profiles)
      Includes index.
      Summary: Profiles the life and career of the former Mouseketeer and popular
young singer, Britney Spears
    ISBN 1-57765-368-8 (hardcover)
    ISBN 1-57765-369-6 (paperback)
    1. Spears, Britney--Juvenile literature. 2. Singers--United States--Biography--
Juvenile literature. [1. Spears, Britney. 2. Singers. 3. Women--Biography.]
I. Title. II. Series.

ML3930.S713 B75 2000
782.42164'092--dc21
   [B]   99-052556

Contents

Britney!

Britney Spears is the music industry's **reigning** teen **diva**. Britney burst onto the music scene in 1999 with her hit album ...*Baby One More Time*. Her strong voice and great dance moves have made Britney a star!

But success did not come overnight. Britney worked hard to develop her skills. When she was young, she practiced singing, took gymnastics lessons, and attended **professional** training schools.

The long hours of practice and study have paid off. Britney's hard work, her desire to succeed, and her family's support have made her the best! Britney's journey to the top began in a tiny town in Louisiana.

Opposite page: Britney in concert. Her sold out tour was one of the most successful of the summer of 1999.

Profile: Britney Spears

Name: Britney Jean Spears

Parents: Jamie and Lynne Spears

Siblings: Brother Bryan and sister Jamie Lynn

Date of Birth: December 2, 1981

Place of Birth: Kentwood, Louisiana

Hair: Brown

Eyes: Brown

Height: 5 feet, 4 inches

Favorite color: Baby blue

Favorite singers: Whitney Houston and Mariah Carey

Favorite TV shows: *Friends* and *Felicity*

Hobbies: Reading and shopping

Young Britney

Britney Jean Spears was born on December 2, 1981. She is the second child of Jamie and Lynne Spears. Jamie is a construction **contractor**. Lynne is an elementary school teacher. Britney has an older brother, Bryan, and a younger sister, Jamie Lynn.

The Spears family lives in Kentwood, Louisiana. Kentwood is about one hour north of New Orleans, near the Mississippi border.

Britney began singing as a very small child. Almost from the time she could talk, Britney could sing and even carry a tune! Soon, she began singing at school, in her church choir, and at other community events. As her **audiences** grew, people began to realize that Britney had a special talent for singing.

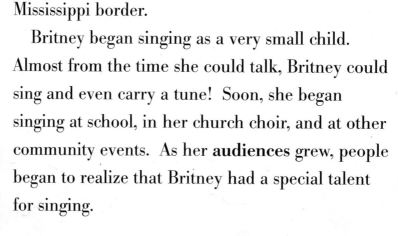

8

*Britney with her mom,
Lynne, at the Teen
Choice Awards.*

A Child Star

When Britney was eight, she heard about an **audition** in Atlanta, Georgia. The Walt Disney Company was looking for kids to star as Mouseketeers on the Disney Channel's *The Mickey Mouse Club* series. Britney and her mother went to Atlanta so Britney could try out for the show.

Britney's talent **impressed** the producers of *The Mickey Mouse Club*. But, Britney was not picked to be a Mouseketeer. They felt she was too young for the show.

But one of the producers thought Britney had the talent to be a star. He suggested that she get in touch with an **agent** in New York City for some **professional** training. Britney's mother was concerned about the family living apart. But soon she agreed to take Britney to New York.

The original Mickey Mouse Club with the creator, Walt Disney, in the middle. Britney Spears had always dreamed of being a member.

HESTER
Library Media Center

New York

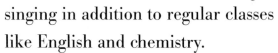

Lynne and Britney spent three summers living in New York City. Britney studied at the Dance Center, an off-Broadway dance training center. She went to school at the Professional Performing Arts School. There, she studied singing in addition to regular classes like English and chemistry.

The **professional** training soon paid off. Britney won parts in commercials for products like Bell South, Days Inn, and Mauls Barbecue Sauce. In 1991, Britney got the lead part in an off-Broadway play called *Ruthless*. In 1992, Britney **performed** twice on the television talent show *Star Search*.

Britney's career was taking shape. Soon, another opportunity to **audition** for *The Mickey Mouse Club* came up. This time, things turned out differently for Britney.

Below: A view of New York City. Opposite page: Britney takes a stroll through New York.

The Mickey Mouse Club

T he producers of *The Mickey Mouse Club* had not forgotten Britney Spears. When she was 11, she was finally hired to be one of 20 Mouseketeers.

Britney was part of a talented group. Other Mouseketeers included *Felicity*'s Keri Russell. JC Chasez and Justin Timberlake from the hit group 'N Sync were Mouseketeers, too.

The Mickey Mouse Club was filmed at Walt Disney World in Orlando, Florida. So, Britney spent half the year in Orlando and the other half at home in

Britney lived half the year in Orlando while she filmed the Mickey Mouse Club at Walt Disney World.

Kentwood. Once again, the family was together only part of the time. But Britney's career was taking off.

The Mickey Mouse Club was canceled after two years. But Britney had discovered that she wanted to be a singer. So she headed back home to Kentwood with an eye on the music business.

Britney hanging out backstage.

Back to New York

In Kentwood, Britney went back to school. She attended Park Lane School in McComb, Mississippi. She was a good student. She liked English and history, but was not as excited about math. But after her success on stage and television, Britney found high school life dull.

Britney decided to return to New York City to work on her music career. Back in New York, Britney **auditioned** for an all-girl singing group. The group was later named Innosense. Lynn Harless, the mother of her pal Justin Timberlake from *The Mickey Mouse Club*, managed it.

Britney did well at the audition, but she decided to **pursue** a solo career. She soon

Britney heads back to New York.

landed an audition at Jive records, label of the supergroups Backstreet Boys and 'N Sync. Britney sang "Jesus Loves Me," and a song by Whitney Houston, "I Have Nothing."

Jive executives recognized Britney's talent. She signed a recording contract.

Britney with the members of the band 'N Synch. Her Mickey Mouse Club pals, Justin Timberlake (to Britney's right in the first photo and to her left in the second photo) and JC Chasez (top right corner in the first photo and to Britney's right in the second photo) are in the band.

Jive

At Jive, Britney began to work on her first album. She worked with **professional** songwriters to write the songs on the album.

After recording the songs for her album, Britney set out on a **promotional** tour. She sang in shopping malls and visited radio stations. She gave interviews and talked to people. She gave fans free copies of her music. It was a tough schedule, but Britney was gaining national recognition.

During this hectic time, Britney added fashion model to her

Britney waves to her fans.

18

impressive list of accomplishments. She signed on to be a model for Tommy Hilfiger. In the middle of this whirlwind of events, Jive released Britney's album.

Britney stops for a photo opportunity at the 1999 Teen Choice Awards.

Success

Britney's album, ...*Baby One More Time*, was released on January 12, 1999. It was an immediate hit. The first single released was the title track, also called "...Baby One More Time." The song **debuted** at number 17 on the *Billboard* chart and kept climbing.

Soon, both the album and the single were in the number one slots on *Billboard*'s charts. It was the first time both a debut album and single had reached *Billboard*'s number one spots at the same time.

...*Baby One More Time* sold enough copies to become quintuple platinum. An album is termed platinum when one million copies are sold. Fans have bought more than five million copies of Britney's smash hit! More than two million

copies were sold in one two-week period alone! When Britney
left New York City, she had decided she wanted a career in
music. She was finally a success!

*Excited fans scream for Britney Spears during her appearance at San
Francisco's Union Square.*

Britney on Tour

Britney began touring as the opening act for 'N Sync. The tour **reunited** her with JC Chasez and Justin Timberlake from her Mouseketeer days.

Many of the fans at the 'N Sync shows were there to see the guys in the band. Most of them had never heard of Britney. But when Britney got on stage and started to sing, she grabbed people's attention. Soon, fans at the shows were cheering for Britney, too!

The second single from ...*Baby One More Time* was released on March 20, 1999. "Sometimes" raced up the charts and landed in the number one spot. With two number one singles from a number one album, Britney was ready to **headline** her own tour.

Opposite page: Britney sings in concert in the summer of 1999.

Moving Right Along

In the summer of 1999, Britney kicked off her own tour. Tommy Hilfiger sponsored the tour. *Teen People* Magazine's fashion designer styled and designed Britney's wardrobe. Her first show was in Pompano Beach, Florida.

Britney's third single was released in August 1999. "(You Drive Me) Crazy" is on the soundtrack of the movie *Drive Me Crazy*. The movie was released in October. Britney is not a newcomer to soundtracks. Her song "Soda Pop" is on the soundtrack to *Sabrina, the Teenage Witch*.

Opposite page: Britney in concert. One of her "looks" during her shows includes a black wig.

Into the Future

Britney is busy working on her second album. She has been writing lots of songs. Look for them on her next album. She will be recording it after she finishes her big tour.

Britney is also still interested in acting. She is working on creating her own television series. She also may guest star on other popular shows.

While Britney has managed to become a successful singing star, she has not ruled out college. Whether it's singing, acting, or studying, Britney Spears is certain to be a huge success!

Opposite page: Britney Spears smiles for the cameras at the 26th annual American Music Awards.

Fun Facts

• Class of '00! Britney attends the University of Nebraska Home School Program. She will graduate from high school in the spring of 2000.

• Britney's high school, Park Lane School, is in McComb, Mississippi. McComb is the hometown of another hip **diva**, pop star Brandy!

• ...*Baby One More Time* is now the top-selling album by a teenage female artist! It has sold more than six million copies, one million more than LeAnn Rimes' 1996 album *Blue*.

How to Contact Britney

Britney's official Web site is:
www.britneyspears.com
Email Britney at:
britney@peeps.com

Britney Spears Fan Club
P. O. Box 7022
Red Bank, NJ 07701-7022

Britney Spears
Jive Records
137-139 West 25th St.
New York, NY 10001

*Britney appearing on
the Tonight Show.*

Glossary

Agent: a person who represents a singer or actor.

Audience: a group of people who watch or listen to a performance.

Audition: a short performance to show ability in order to get a part in a movie, a play, or a band.

Contractor: a person who agrees to furnish materials and perform services at an agreed upon price.

Debut: the first appearance.

Diva: a leading female singer.

Headline: to be the main attraction at a concert, movie, or play.

Impress: to affect someone strongly.

Perform: to present entertainment to an audience.

Professional: possessing great skill or experience in a field or activity.

Promotional: advertising, publicity, or public relations. Something given away for free on a promotional tour is called a promo.

Pursue: to try to obtain or accomplish something.

Reign: to have authority or importance.

Reunite: to bring things or people back together again.

Pass It On

Tell readers around the country information you've learned about your favorite superstars. Share your little-known facts and interesting stories.
We want to hear from you!
To get posted on the ABDO Publishing Company Web site
email us at: Adventure@abdopub.com
Download a free screen saver at www.abdopub.com

Index